Golf Widows

ANGUS
& ROBERTSON
PUBLISHERS

Golf Widows
A Survival Course
Foreword by Alan Coren

Noel Ford

ANGUS & ROBERTSON PUBLISHERS

Unit 4, Eden Park, 31 Waterloo Road,
North Ryde, NSW, Australia 2113, and
16 Golden Square, London W1R 4BN,
United Kingdom.

First published in the United Kingdom
by Angus & Robertson (UK) in 1988
First published in Australia by
Angus & Robertson Publishers in 1988

Typeset by New Faces, Bedford
Printed in Great Britain by
Richard Clay Plc, Bungay, Suffolk

British Library Cataloguing in Publication Data
Ford, Noel
    Golf widows – a survival course.
    1. English wit and humor, Pictorial
    I. Title
    741.5'942   NC1479

ISBN: 0 207 15814 2 hardback
ISBN: 0 207 15958 0 paperback (not available in the UK)

Foreword
by Alan Coren

Had you, a week or so ago, been taking a sundown stroll through the rolling Bucks verdure, you might have seen, some four or so miles from Amersham, a strange misshapen silhouette blemishing the evening horizon. There on a busty hill it stood, rooted: a gnarled thorn, you might have said to yourself, shrugging; a Saxon barrow, time-tumbled; an extravagant horse-dropping, piled and eroded by the Chiltern wind.

Had you time on your hands, you might have gone closer. Ah, you might have cried, a statue of Charles Laughton raised by the Gerrards Cross Victor Hugo Society! That fearsome hump, those twisted legs, that shoulder dropping unnervingly to the knee, counterpointing the movement of that horrible head as it wrenches unnaturally upward to poke its pitiful eye at the uncaring stars, what could it be but the great hunchback himself, frozen forever by the sculptor's art?

It could be me practising my swing, that's what. As, indeed, it was. The fact that the figure displayed not a tremor of movement is explained by its having been practising this swing for upwards of three hours; and it had slowly come to a complete halt. Indeed, if some charitable Samaritan had not come by and fortunately found the scruff of its neck, the figure might have been there still, a topographical conundrum fit to rank with Stonehenge and the White Horse of Uffington, and a beacon for errant gliders.

That the Samaritan was in fact a lady charged by her howling children to desert her charred beef and track down the bastard upon whose waiting cutlery the tarnish was now forming an unsightly crust will explain much of my unease at what follows.

For Noel Ford has got it all horribly – and hilariously – right.

A golf course is a Pilgrim's Progress, an analogue of man's travail and aspiration. Perfectability is held out, not because it is achievable, but because it is a grail to be striven for; the Good Man is one who devotes himself unwaveringly to self-improvement, driven on by a distant golden promise.

Right, said God, sitting back on the Seventh Day, restless in His rest after a week's hard graft at the ethereal office, I'll call it Sunday, and I'll give them golf. They will all start imperfect, and I shall send them out with their imperfections, and I shall give them sand-traps and water hazards and all manner of obstacles, and as soon as they are getting good, and touched with pride, I shall chuck in something new to lay them low. Man shall trudge the courses of the earth, in fair weather and foul, and be tested at every tree and rough and bit that lies just six inches outside the ropes. Thus, though he may never become perfect, it is in his striving that he shall become Good.

All of which would have been fine, something Man could have handled, had God not subsequently allowed a deep sleep to fall upon Adam (doubtless as the result of his having worn himself out in the bunker at Eden's notorious dog-leg fourth), looked thoughtfully at the bag of snoring bones, and selected therefrom a Number 3 rib.

The rib was the biggest obstacle of all. The rib was the worst thing to happen to golf since God created crosswind. The rib brought handicap into the world, and all our woe. Without the rib, Adam would never have infringed the rules; without the rib, Adam would still be in the club.

But then again, without the rib, Noel Ford would not have been able to offer us this delicious portfolio. For these drawings are all about the eternal war between golfer and golfee; they are full of observation, full of experience, full of truth, and, most important of all, they are full of fun.

Why, even the ribs may be a little tickled.

Round 1:
Classic Symptoms

"Why did you have to give us that bloody apple?"

"No, he's not here ... we think he may be visiting his wife."

"Your father's getting his company car today so at least tonight the main topic of conversation won't be golf!"

"We still argue. He says this is Heaven but I say it's Hell!"

Even our lawn's made up of divots from Carnoustie,
St Andrew's, Gleneagles ..."

"The message in the bottle ... it got through!"

"Do you mind if I play through? I have to get to court to stop my wife from divorcing me."

"… *square up your shoulders at the address, parallel to the target line, make a 90° shoulder turn while the hands and arms swing the club up and …*"

"*Give him his toys back this minute!*"

"I didn't suspect that he'd gone missing until I noticed, the other day, that these were still in the house."

"... and if you hear noises in the night and you see a strange man carrying a bag over his shoulder, it'll probably be Daddy."

*"Of course I haven't forgotten our anniversary, dear
... why, only just now we were drinking your health."*

*Look, I know the club doesn't divulge members'
addresses ... I'm just asking you to remind me of mine!"*

"He's got his father's swing!"

"My Best Man must have filled it with confetti after the service this afternoon."

"So much for the giant leap forward his invention of the
club was supposed to bring!"

"Oh no! ... not another of Jim's golfing pals!"

"Haven't you caught anything for dinner yet?"

"Think carefully. When he said he'd meet you at
St Andrews …"

"… and the one day a year you aren't playing, you're out God knows where all night!"

Round 2:
Remedial Action

"My wife's claiming I'm unfaithful and naming the entire membership as co-respondents in the divorce."

"Take this golf-bag home."

"You live and breathe it … I figured you might as well eat it!"

*"Goodnight, Cynthia. I trust I've heard the last of this
'I'm leaving you' rubbish ..."*

"Here come our wives! Quick, pretend to be looking at the Girlie-mags."

"Here he comes now. You won't be too rough with him, will you?"

"Look here, Wilson, the other members would
appreciate it if your wife expressed her grievances
away from the club."

"No, it's not another new-fangled shape putter. My wife
clobbered me over the head with it."

"Harry disappeared into the rough twenty minutes ago
… we think his wife must have ambushed him."

"… so then she said, 'Why should I have to stay at
home all the time looking after the baby?'"

"Damn'd wife put superglue in the blasted hole!"

"No, I'm afraid Jerry won't be able to make up your foursome after all."

"His wife's hidden his clubs again."

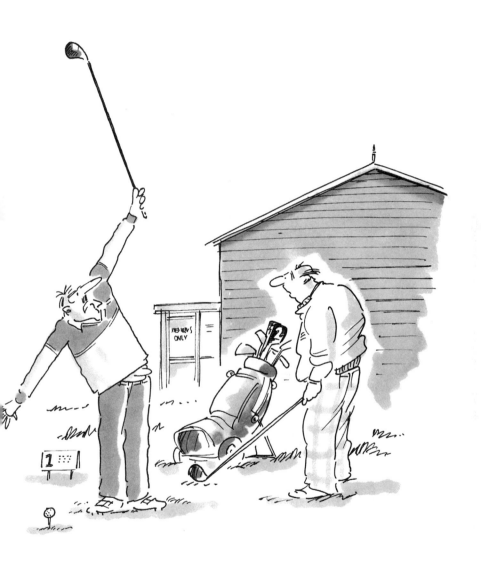

"She must be mad at me. She's starched my
sweater again."

"Dammit, Julia, don't be so spiteful."

"It's a par 68 from the golf-club to his house."

"She lets me go golfing on Sundays as long as I caddy
for her on Saturdays."

"Mind you, she's fair. She lets him play a full nine holes before she reels him in."

*"If you can't sleep, try counting the number of strokes
it took you to get out of that bunker today."*

"Helen! … have you been tampering with my
Practice-Putter again?"

"Okay, Mum … he's addressing the ball … NOW!"

*"Poor Devil ... after the divorce his wife got custody
of the golf clubs."*

"He's been getting round much quicker since I started slipping laxative into his hip-flask."

"We have plenty of time. I bent George's driver and it will take him ages to get round."

"If there's a golf-club in the afterlife, you'll never get through to him."

"He's lucky. If she'd been really mad, she'd have used the other end of it."

GOLF CLUB
Pro Shop

Round 3:
Relapse

"Hello, dear ... had a nice day? ... new outfit, is it?"

*"Mavis! For pity's sake! I'm trying to keep my eye
on the ball."*

*"Damn the woman ... I'd normally get down in one
from here."*

"How many shots did it take you, dear?"

*"My wife says if I don't cut down on golf, she's going on
sex-strike ... whatever sex is."*

"Fetch!"

"The committee has responded remarkably quickly ... changing this from a par three to four."

"Looks like Sandra wants me home early again."

"I love her when she's angry. She puts 75 yards on my drive."

"Agatha! ... Can't this wait until after dinner with the club president and his wife?"

"Sandra must have moved the tee marker ... this'll put
another fifty yards on the hole!"

*"Hello George ... listen, something awful has happened.
Eric was supposed to be partnering me in this
afternoon's tournament ..."*

"Oh, hello, dear. Any sign of my ball from up there?"

"Do you mind if I go first? ... I'm late for my game
as it is."

"Oh, ignore her ... it's only my wife."

"Fore!"

"Muriel! Please! Not with my best driver!"

*"Good Lord, isn't that Frobisher? ... his wife said he
was away on a business trip."*

*"Hmm ... sliced it, but not a bad drive under
the circumstances."*

*"Oh, yes, he's been a great help around the house since
I had him stuffed."*

"Aren't women funny? One day they're complaining about your golf, the next they're digging a practice-bunker for you in the garden."

*"I don't think she minds too much about all the golf.
Why, only today, she gave me this lovely new sweater."*

"Henry got those for golfing and I got that for shooting."

"Frankly, madam, you over-reacted. A seven-iron would have done the trick."

"For heaven's sake, dear! Your grip's all wrong!"

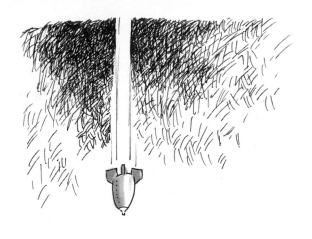

"Things are much better at home, now that Hilda has a hobby. She's taking flying lessons."

"This stuff really cut down on the housework. I put it in my husband's coffee."

"I didn't know we'd commissioned a statue."